It's Your Decision

It's Your Decision

◆

An Alternate Step

Danny Rhodes

iUniverse, Inc.
New York Lincoln Shanghai

It's Your Decision
An Alternate Step

Copyright © 2006 by Danny carl Rhodes

iUniverse books may be ordered through booksellers or by contacting:

iUniverse
2021 Pine Lake Road, Suite 100
Lincoln, NE 68512
www.iuniverse.com
1-800-Authors (1-800-288-4677)

ISBN-13: 978-0-595-39782-2 (pbk)
ISBN-13: 978-0-595-84189-9 (ebk)
ISBN-10: 0-595-39782-4 (pbk)
ISBN-10: 0-595-84189-9 (ebk)

Printed in the United States of America

Dedicated to the strength and perseverance

of my loving wife

Vicki

and children

Matthew, Amanda, and Caryn

and all the family that stuck by and believed in me

and

a special thanks to

Christina

for the counseling, encouragement

and never ending support

Contents

Preface

Alcoholism. As we continue to grow in our lifetime, we will always be facing life's challenges. How large these challenges are is what I consider a frame of mind. Take about any question and present it to two people at the same time and see what answers you receive. Try it with two men, two women, an adult and a child, a man and a woman, two people with different ethnic backgrounds. Do the math and you will find the combinations of people are almost endless, along with the answers you will receive to the same question. Now ask each group of these two people to work together and come up with one answer. Now ask all the different groups to get together and form one answer.

Who do we choose to come up with the right answers? What is a right answer? An answer should be the solution to a problem. Have we found all the solutions to all the problems? Is it really a problem that is being dealt with, or an unanswered question? Isn't it all how one perceives the challenge? Regardless of the answers you receive, not everybody will agree it's the right one. Majority will always rule and determine the "right" answer to put on paper.

Our right answer is the one that satisfies our own needs, no matter what the right answer is on paper. As we perceive challenges differently, then the answers will also be different. Facing the world of alcoholism brings up questions with as large an answer base as there is a combination of people and how they perceive the challenge. Having faced this challenge myself, I found that this particular challenge, at this particular time, has very few answers.

We rely on what is written on paper for a cure. Some will tell you there is no cure and you will always be an alcoholic. This is where I beg to differ.

My views and opinions are just that. Mine. I do not profess to have years of medical degrees or psychiatric counseling training. I have my own opinions. I express them the way I feel comfortable with, so if you find the language sometimes rude or vulgar, along with my opinions or comments, I apologize in advance. I call a spade a spade. I never could figure out why there is a the problem of whether the glass is half full or half empty. If you are pouring into it, you are in the process of filling, so it's half full. Right? If it's being drank, you are in the process of emptying, so it's half empty. Right? If you just walked into the room and saw this glass, there is no answer. Incomplete information which requires research. So here we are discussing alcoholism. My thoughts on how to deal with alcoholism worked for me. It may or may not work for you, but if you are reading this, then you probably haven't found the answer for yourself or a loved one close to you living with this challenge. Yet.

"You gain strength, courage and confidence by every experience in which you really stop to look fear in the face......You must do the thing you think you cannot do."

—Eleanor Roosevelt, American First Lady (1884–1962)

1

Take your time reading this. You will not be tested in the morning, nor am I going to challenge your literacy by big fancy words used by authors of noble importance. I am not of noble importance to anyone except my family, and not even to all of them. Nor am I a literary genius that can come up with those four dollar words anyways.

What I have to say and how I say it is explained in the preface. Despite all the years of training and schooling the brains of this world have gone through, the countless dollars spent on education, the time spent on research, etc., they still may not find all the answers to all the problems. That doesn't make the problem go away, they just need to dig a little deeper. Every minute that is spent on research without results leads to more people getting caught up in the problem. If we don't find all the answers and the problem won't go away, where does that leave us? I don't think that certain situations are always looked at thoroughly enough, or all the different angles covered. In the studies of alcoholism, where does the system stand? It seems to me that the system doesn't stand too well on that issue, we don't seem to be lacking in out-of-control drinkers, better known as alcoholics. Progress made in the last four decades to our lifestyle has been staggering. But what will come tomorrow?

What makes me feel that I can discuss this issue with any backbone? The simple fact is I have done what they say can't be done. I conquered my alcoholism. My way. Can you? Sure you can. And never let them tell you that it is impossible. I think that issue is what gets us in trouble in the first place. That issue is letting someone or some group of people influence what we think and do. That is the whole point of this writing. If you truly believe you can break alcoholism, then you can. As a matter of fact, if you put your mind to it, you can accomplish just about anything. Simple theory as it is, but of course there are always going to be complications, and exceptions. Did you ever think that something as complex as alcoholism can be conquered with a change in one's way of thinking? Has this approach really been thoroughly investigated? All anybody needs in that situation is a proper attitude and determination with a little support. I obviously didn't sprout extra brain cells recently, so I just figured out how to use the brains I have to my best advantage to achieve the results I wanted. What I wanted was to break the cycles of a typical alcoholic. Either that or I was going to die. Or kill someone.

2

When I first decided to write this I'd have a tough time sleeping, thinking about how to start this, what to say, how to say it. I'd wake up and my mind would be going a mile a minute. I am not a writer. I never took journalism, so I am sure I will be criticized not only in the context of my ideas but my writing style as well. I am writing this book the way I want to, the way I would talk to you face to face. I am simply here to talk, not preach or teach. I think it's fickle when people try to be something they are not. Nobody has all the answers, but some will have experience in the situation you are faced with. Some have been there, done that, and can relate the obstacles they encountered to you. Nobody is perfect, and putting on a false front doesn't cut it with me. For instance, I was at a church one time and two women were discussing a church function and apparently were averse to how it was being run. I overheard one of the gals say she thought it was a bunch of BS. Why would she bother saying BS? Is it because they were in a church? Sure. But the thing is, everybody knows what BS means. It's not Boy Scouts. It's not Barbeque Sauce. It's BullShit. Whether you said bullshit or BS, you said it. You may as well come out and say it if everybody knows what you are saying anyways. And this is how I'm writing this book. I say what I mean. Even though I try to be civil and non slanderous, some of you will take offense. Tough cookies. Get over it.

3

Amazingly, as I sat down to write, it struck me. Our local newspaper has been following the Lewis and Clark expedition by daily excerpts from their diaries and yesterday (200 years ago) they reached the Pacific Ocean. It's not that a white man had never been on the Pacific Northwest coast, it's just that they had never reached it from this direction. A direct land route rather than sailing around to it. Any destination can be achieved in many ways and one method for one may not be the best or successful at all for another. It takes guts and determination to try a new course to accomplish what needs to be done. But without someone being versatile enough to try something new, all possible routes may not be discovered, leaving a few behind. When it comes to alcoholism, those few are more like tens of thousands. They just can't get there, or disagree with the current recommended methods of recovery.

This is where I stir up controversy. Do not get me wrong. I am in full support of Alcoholics Anonymous and what they can and have accomplished. But not everyone in this world is a believer in higher powers, God, faith in religion. Or maybe they were believers but are angry and feel as though these higher powers have let them down creating the ugly situation they are in. Very seldom will you get an alcoholic to accept the responsibilities of their actions; they are usually "victims of their environment."

You see, just about everyday I read of a new breakthrough in technology, medical advancements, new methods of applied thinking, etc. When a new drug is a major breakthrough for an illness, they find it can also work for (or better) a totally dissociated illness or disease. Many of these are found by pure accident years later. The thing is, it seems to be a complacency of solving a problem, only to find there can be multiple solutions to the same problem. There may also be several different problems that may be resolved with one solution. We seem to quit looking after we have found a solution to a situation.

4

Haven't you noticed that when a new "whatchamacallit" is produced, it's a mad dash to copy and improve on it, with very few looking for new "whatchamacallits"? These new technical wonders are quite often thought up by unknowns. I'm going to call them unknowns, because these people don't have degrees on the wall, nor are they afraid to look like idiots amongst their peers. Their peers do not have a "Haaaaavaaad" degree on the wall, thus they are not afraid to embarrass themselves in front of them. The sad part is, once an unknown comes up with an idea, it's the "papered" people that usually take the ideas and run with them. They will be rewarded with the fame and fortune that goes with it.

I happen to be one of those unknowns that stumbled on to a solution to a challenge. The challenge of alcoholism. The same way I stumbled into the challenge itself. Unknowingly and unprepared. The thing is, I don't have one of those fancy degrees on the wall, yet I feel that I possess something that a whole lot of those brains don't have. A bit of common sense. My brain is not filled with all the technical crap that is required to solve problems. One of the things I figured out was, there are different types of problems that require different approaches for a solution. Two plus two is a problem. For a solution you can take two apples, set them beside two more apples, then count them together. You get four apples. Simple math. Alcoholism is a problem. You cannot take any amount of alcoholics and stand them by another amount of alcoholics, and come up with a solution. Period. So where do we get the complacency to stick with the only solution that we know of so far?

5

There is a columnist that I must admit I don't read too often. If I plan on writing again, I guess I'd better start. The man is wise. I read a column of his just a few weeks ago that had caught my eye. His name is James Kilpatrick. This particular column is about a woman whose husband died of cancer and she was awarded $55 million dollars from a major tobacco company. I think you will see a similarity. The jury contended that he died from said tobacco company "fraudulently marketing a defective product". I don't believe that the cigarettes were defective, they did their job they were produce to do, nor do I believe they were sold fraudulently. In the good old days, they were unaware of the dangers of smoking. The Native Americans had been doing it for years before we even got here, so there was nothing to be warned about at the time. As signs started to point cancer in the direction of cigarettes, warnings about the hazards of smoking on each pack of cigarettes he smoked started to appear. As this column goes on, it was with the opinion that "…it's basically a case of a predictable death resulting from the pure blind stupidity of a man who didn't have the willpower to quit 40 years ago." Well put Mr Kilpatrick, the same goes with alcohol.

This column goes on to state that cigarettes do indeed cause cancer, not in all smokers, but in up to a third of them. I wonder what the percentage of alcoholics is to anyone that has drank alcohol?

I have known a few families that cancer runs rampant, yet none of them smoke. Alcohol is not a defective product. It's the use and abuse of it that gets people killed. Should a motorcycle manufacturer be liable if a rider gets their brains knocked out because he or she didn't wear a helmet? How do we know if we are allergic to a particular food? We eat it and something bad happens. If we survive, and are wise, we don't eat it again. So you buy your first born kid their first candy bar. NOW you find out they are allergic to peanuts and the kid dies on the way to the hospital. Do you sue the peanut pickers of the world, the packager, the distributors? How far do we go with this?

6

Alcoholics Anonymous was created in the 1930's. Their method of treatment requires one to turn themselves over to a higher power. Being in an alcohol treatment program twice myself, hospitalized, detox, the whole nine yards, I was forced to attend AA meetings. There was no option by law. At first I was open to see what they had to offer. Actually closer to say I was at least interested to see what AA was all about. It did not fit my needs or beliefs. I was told by three different counselors that AA does not force religion down your throat, yet at each meeting the entire class was asked to hold hands in a circle and repeat the serenity prayer. The very first word in the prayer is GOD. My personal religious beliefs are private to me, I don't discuss religion. I don't get opinionated against others for their beliefs or how they wish to express them. I just feel it's a private thing. Even my health care provider at the time dropped me because I would not go through the program again and be subjected to hours of religious bombardment and negative thinking. I always wondered if they could legally "fire" me, but they did. Of course with most health care providers it's about money, not health. This will be among the topics if I write another book later. I guess they figured I couldn't handle my alcoholism my way so they didn't want to pay for me puking out on them. This is where the system falls short for many people.

We can realize that when AA was formed in the 1930's, most people were in the "Little House on the Prairie" mode. Everyone knew everybody else in town, and they all went to the same church on Sunday. But this is today. We are in a 24/7 life. People work on Sunday.

Remember when the video game "Pong" came out? Man that was technology. Look at the computer games now. Remember when it was "one nation, under God..."? Look at the way we now separate church and state to be politically correct and not offend certain people. There are people today trying to replace the word Christmas with Holiday. Should we not look at alcoholism in the same way? Eventually the methods to deal with alcoholism will need to be updated to fit today's lifestyle and beliefs.

This seems to be a system that still believes that the AA way is the only way. My way by the law of averages will fail. That's what they say. But who are they and what the hell do they know? Have they been to the bottom of a whiskey bottle? Probably not. Some may have. Most came from a preppy school that taught them one method of dealing with the problem. Only recently has the system devoted more time to find the medical quirks the brain goes through under a chemical disturbance, and ways to deal with it through medication. Remember what I said about a different pathway to a destination? The only way that I got to my destination was by the flexibility of my rehab counselor. I think she figured out real soon that I was part mule and wanted to handle things my way. You see, I'm different. I didn't belong there. Sound familiar? I soon found out that everybody thought they were different and didn't belong there.

7

Not all counselors are that flexible, and she continued to educate us as to what we were doing to ourselves and the people around us, both mentally and physically. What's funny (not really) is that when you enter a rehab program, you are assessed to determine the intensity and length of your particular rehab time. What they need to do is determine the TYPE of treatment necessary to be successful. What's bad about that is you have to pay the assessor money to do that, when in fact that is what the judge told us we had to do. You see, there are all kinds of alcoholics, and they need to be treated accordingly. There are first timers who just plain made a mistake. There are repeat offenders and there are also the ones with medical or mental problems.

One major thing that bothers me about AA is that people are never successful, which is what I meant about the negativity in an AA meeting. To AA, you are always going to be an alcoholic, in recovery. "HI, My name is Mary and I'm an alcoholic." Hi Mary. "Hi, my name is Ted and I'm an alcoholic" Hi Ted. This is the way I look at it. My name is Dan, and I'm an EX-alcoholic. If I call myself a dog enough times, I'll grow a tail and start barking. If I call myself an alcoholic enough times, I'll be thoroughly convinced I am and remain that way. Who you are and what you are should be determined by one individual. You. The health care provider I had at the time predetermined that I was going to fail. Don't you think that was a poor time in my life to be dropped? And they have the balls enough to call themselves health care providers. What a joke.

8

Can you spot an alcoholic? What if I were to show up at an AA meeting for the first time and tell everybody that I was only there to gather information for a friend or family member that is an alcoholic? At that point, they only see me as a person without a drinking problem. What if I should walk into that meeting and tell everybody that I am one of three things. One is that I am an alcoholic, two is I never drank alcohol in my life, or three, I'm an Ex-alcoholic? We can figure right off the bat they will pooh-pooh the idea of an ex-alcoholic because as far as they are concerned, we can only reach the in-recovery stage. It's like a wall has been put up that you hit head-on, and that's as far as you can get. I do think it's kind of neat that Alcoholics Anonymous honors their members with progress tokens though. They are the coins stamped with the different lengths of time being sober. It gives people incentive to reach the next level, something to shoot for. But think about it. Let's say one person has a one week coin and their buddy has a ten year coin and they go out together and get hammered drunk, who is the biggest loser there? As far as I'm concerned they have both failed. Equally. Could you match the coin with the person if you had just met them for the first time?

I guess now comes the $64,000 question. Who failed? The individual, AA, or the higher power?

9

We are taught by sages. We are taught by people that have been there and done that. We are also taught speculation, unknown but by the law of averages should work this way. We are taught by our parents, who were taught by their parents. Most of everything taught today is the same old crap we've known for ages. In this respect our knowledge is limited to what we know already. Too few individuals get outside the comfort zone of knowledge to seek answers. It is true we have literally thousands of researchers and scientists working hard to advance our society and prolong our life, but if you think about it, they all came from the same schools. Knowledge gained is either passed around or stolen, then disbursed to all the schools for all of mankind to share. These people can spend an hour lecturing about or write a book on the theory and relevance of why we need a license plate on our cars, but they probably don't know what a phillips screwdriver is or why this tool is necessary to accomplish mounting these plates on our cars. The people that show us the way are taught at these schools. There are a lot of smart people in this world, and just because they didn't go to these schools and get that piece of paper that says they are smart, they will seldom be heard.

How long has this planet been in existence? Millions of years, as far as they can speculate. How long has man been on this planet? This depends on your personal beliefs. Let's just say a really, really long time. Of all the time that this planet has been in existence and man been alive, we have discovered only about 500 years ago that the earth was round. That's pretty basic knowledge for the time we've been here.

I see so much time, effort and money in research and testing for the recovery of alcohol addiction. Are we sure we have found all the routes to deal with this situation? We spend millions of dollars in research to find the technical mumbo jumbo that causes alcohol addiction, but what if you could convince someone they can beat it by themselves? That is, basically by simply talking themselves out of the thinking that they are alcoholics. Rich boy or poor boy. Who will grow up to be the president? An astronaut? CEO of a major company? And which boy will be the garbage man or the bum in the ditch with an empty wine bottle. Rich man or poor man. Who is the smartest? Dress them the same and put them side by side and let them answer the same question. Just because the rich man will be more educated, he will have more of the right answers. Remember that one of those right answers claimed the world was flat, so what if these right answers aren't correct? The right answer is what they say it should be, based on the knowledge handed down. Maybe if they didn't have their brains so crammed with knowledge they could think.

Speaking of money, is that not what is responsible for so many broken marriages? A lot of people turn to alcoholism because they are poor and are not satisfied with the conditions they are living in. What would happen if there was no money? People would have to find something else to do with their time besides argue and fight. It would be one less excuse to drink. So what does this have to do with you? Money is a given. I don't see us living in a Star Trek society soon. The money situation as it stands will probably still be in existence by the time we die. So instead of giving all our efforts in trying to change it, we need to focus on how to handle the situation we are in now. A not so lucky addicted gambler will soon run out of money, but if he stops long enough, he will get the money saved back up. What if this money is focused somewhere else that achieves different results? His gambling didn't get him the results he wanted, although it was fun at the time he was doing it. Your drinking didn't work out worth a damn as far as end results are concerned, but it was fun when you did it. Right? Funny thing is, we can look at a gambler as being an idiot because all they need to do is keep their money in their pockets. That gambler is looking at an out of control alcoholic as an idiot, because all the alcoholic has to do is pick up a soft drink instead of booze. They are still building Casinos, and they are still making alcohol. It's your decision to walk through the Casino doors and order a drink, or not.

10

Current forms of counseling put little faith in people as far as I can tell. Take for example; AA does not believe that an individual has the will-power or focus available to control themselves in their surroundings or how they are going to deal with them. This can be yet another injection of negativity that we can't accomplish self control, leading us to believe we will fail again. If I were to go up to somebody involved with AA and told them I was going to meet some friends at a tavern, you'd be able to see the gears grinding and hear their thinking that it can not be anything but trouble. Remember, just because someone else doesn't have the confidence in you, you can still have confidence in yourself. Anything we do in life is our decision. We live with the consequences. Frankly I don't see any harm in sucking down an ice cold soft drink and shooting some pool with friends at a tavern, but I guarantee that's not what would be going through their mind. This is especially important to people who smoke cigarettes. Why not enjoy yourself? The local tavern is about the only place that allows smoking indoors as a public establishment, and even that is changing. If an individual starts drinking again due to the allures of their surroundings, then it's obvious they have not made the full commitment required to cease their alcoholic ways in the first place. The front door swings both ways. If you can't handle the temptation, you can leave. At least you gave it a shot, and not shied away because they told you that you couldn't do it. Maybe you can't. Now. What is the difference in temptation between being at the grocery store, walking down the beer aisle (and/or hard liquor in some states) and being in a tavern?

Granted there is a difference between watching somebody right in front of you drinking and having a good time as opposed to walking down the beer aisle in a store. Yet, what do we see on television or a rented movie in our own home?

Have you ever seen the movie "Arthur"? The whole story was about a spoiled alcoholic. It was funny. I love it. Unfortunately, life isn't like the movies. In real life, we would be pulled over and sent to jail if we drove absolutely hammered like Arthur did. When I got pulled over the first time I guarantee it wasn't like the movies. It was not cute, nor was it funny. This is where your commitment and focus has to take over. Of the 100 plus channels on my television available to watch, I'd bet there is no more than three channels that disallow any smoking, drinking, profanity or nudity of some type. It's a fact of life. Get used to it. Putting blinders on won't help. Even though these are temptations that may be capable of leading you astray, we are surrounded by them and we cannot change it. So that is where a true change of attitude and commitment has to become second nature to you without alcohol even entering your mind in order to have a good time. A good AA member will tell you that you can't go to a tavern. You are surrounded with too much temptation. But who are they to tell you what you can and cannot do? Do they know your psyche? Do you not control your own destiny? Yes you do. Or should.

11

How do I know it can be done? Because I did it myself. Does this make me a superman? Nope. Just me. Our high school graduating class kind of skipped our 30th reunion, so they tried to get together for a massive 50th birthday party being as how most of us were that age. This was just a few months ago. It was a three day event. The second night consisted of meeting at a restaurant downtown that had a separate bar in it, so I guess you can figure out which part we were in. I met up with some of the old drinking buddies from way back when. They were right about where I left them 30 years ago, still doing their best to stand upright, just a little fatter and grayer, with a drink in their hand. I ordered a Coke. My best friend from school was there and we hung together just like the good old days. When we were done for the night, I had 2 Cokes, he had 2 beers. This was in fact the first time I had subjected myself to an environment that the main purpose for being there was to drink alcohol. As the little gal came up and asked what we wanted to drink the first time, I couldn't believe that the words "Rum and Coke" didn't come out of my mouth. My best buddy and I had drunk gallons of that stuff.

We used to find Coke on sale. Of course there was a limited quantity you could buy, so we would make about three or four laps through the store during the day and stack them up in a pyramid at my place. Then we would scrape up the money we had left and run to the liquor store for the rum.

The later the night got, the more I realized what an idiot I used to be. To watch and listen to the old classmates getting hammered drunk, and realize that used to be me made me glad I wasn't that way anymore. I thought of the hangover I would not have tomorrow. I didn't have to worry about getting home, I wasn't drunk behind the wheel.

You say you can drink because from now on you will make sure that you have someone else to drive. Right. After three or four beers you realize there isn't any more in the fridge. The kid probably drank some of it behind your back. The store is only a few blocks away, and there is no one around to drive you. It wouldn't hurt to jump in the car real quick and get some more beer. You get away with it. Right on. So what's the difference between a few blocks, a half mile, or maybe only a mile? If you get away with one stupid mistake, you just might get gutsier the next time. Now I will get to see the kids off to school instead of waking up to the major CLANK as they open up my jail cell for breakfast. You can't believe the looks I would get when people saw that I was drinking a Coke. Straight Coke. They weren't used to seeing that out of me. I was usually the first one to hit the staggering stage at all the parties. A couple of them felt my forehead to see if I had a serious fever or something. But you know what? I still had a great time. And I could have kicked their ass at the pool table because they were probably seeing two cue balls to poke the stick at and try to hit. The next day was a get together at a park. Most of my buddy's eyes were bleeding, and they were moving real slow. I felt great. I was glad it was them and not me. Because I had been there, done that. I just laughed at them. The way others used to laugh at me. I'm glad I made my decision not to be that way anymore.

12

One more thing about the common method of thinking behind alcohol recovery is the distancing of yourself and the friends you used to drink with. A lot of these people have been our friends for years, and if they can't understand that you wish not to drink alcohol anymore as your choice and it makes them uncomfortable, then they weren't really your friends anyways. I am a firm believer that it is possible to have friends that drink and I don't. Why should I have to break off a long term friendship just because they drink and I don't? I say that they are welcome to drink in my home and socialize the way they are comfortable without the worry of tempting me to join in the fun or insulting me. It's like a loveless marriage, constant pressure. The guests feel obligated to change their ways in front of you, and if that makes them uncomfortable, they won't be coming around. There is always a tension being careful not to offend the other people in the room. This in turn makes you feel guilty because you are the reason they are not enjoying themselves. This may also create a desire to drink again to salvage your friendship. Think about it. If a dear friend died due to an accident or illness, you would be devastated. If you lost this same friend over the fact you couldn't be around them just because they drink alcohol, it would be no less devastating. They are still gone. As a matter of fact, cutting them out of your life is the same as causing the accident responsible for them being dead. They are to you now.

We don't need any more guilt trips. We caused enough damage to ourselves already. A loss is a loss. So why would you want to subject yourself to the loss because you don't have the self confidence to be around drinkers after choosing to live your life without alcohol? Haven't you suffered enough in the fact that you have already driven friends and/or family members away because of your previous alcohol induced actions? I believe that your surroundings are what are going to make you successful in your quest for sobriety. Totally leaving family and friends behind closed doors and starting fresh is a scary idea. You need support. You need at least some of the comfort zone surroundings in order to not shock and overwhelm yourself with change. Overwhelming yourself with change may induce a sense of inability to control your situation, thus setting yourself up for failure. Have you ever jumped out of a scorching hot sauna into a cold lake? It's your decision as to how you want to handle your total break from alcoholism. If you really are not confident enough and feel like you do need a total change, then do it. But don't let them tell you a total break is required for your success. The only thing that is required for success is what works for you, regardless what the law of averages say is required to be successful. You are an individual.

If you know that eating rat poison is bad, and a juicy prime rib steak is good, then you have the common sense to know where alcohol fits in your life. If drinking the alcohol didn't work to your expectations or satisfaction, then don't do it. It's your decision what to eat. It's your decision what to drink. It's your decision. Period.

When I train a puppy, I will smack it on the ass with a rolled up newspaper when it does something bad, and reward it when it has done something good. We already did something bad by abusing our liberties with alcohol. We've been punished enough. We don't need anymore, and deleting our past friends is what I consider a form of punishment. They didn't do anything wrong, we did. Did they offer you a drink? You can say no, because you know what the consequences are. If they offered a bare wire plugged into the wall socket, are you going to grab it? Odds are your not going to because you know the consequences of that would be that you would get the dog snot zapped out of you. Keep in mind. If someone offers you a bare wire plugged into a wall socket, they are not your friend. They are the ones you need to distance yourself from. We should be rewarding ourselves for breaking our bad habits, not continuing to punish.

13

A very close friend got me to thinking about something. She asked me a question that I am not only unqualified to answer, but in all my days of being counseled I never heard this question come up. But it did get me to thinking. She asked me "What is the failure rate of AA?" I'm afraid this is where I can stir up even more controversy, like hitting a bees nest with a big rock, and it may sound like I am attacking AA. Not so. Again, I am all for Alcoholics Anonymous and what they have accomplished for so many people, yet their thinking and mine differs greatly. My opinion is that if a person goes back to an alcoholic state, they have failed. If they have to return over and over, day in and day out for the same problem, they have failed. My views are simply this. I look at alcoholism as an illness to be compared to the common cold. I feel there are so many strains of alcoholism that it cannot be cured with one certain pill, neither can a cold. Yet, as with a common cold, no matter how bad we feel for a few days, we get over it, our body shook it. I know that I have had colds bad enough I wanted to die. I got over them. I know I fell into an alcoholic state and could have died, or killed someone. I got over it also. If I wish to get a nasty cold again, I'll kiss someone who has one. If I choose to go back to my alcoholic ways, I'll go buy me a bottle of booze and drink it. These are informed decisions because I have done both and I know the consequences. Although it is true you can catch a cold by someone sneezing their germs all over you at no fault of your own, a drunken person cannot sneeze on you and make you an alcoholic. That's your decision.

14

Yesterday I watched the last race of the NASCAR season on TV. I used to kick up dust at the local speedway for about 13 years. Racing is one of those things you have a tough time getting out of your system. Although my wife and two daughters were in the room, I felt very alone. You see, I also have a son. He grew up and moved out. He was our first born, pretty much what most men want when they get over the shock of the wife being pregnant the first time, a son. Someone who you can raise in your own spitting image and share every aspect of your life, get him to grow up liking the things you like. When my son was born, I was still racing and playing music. When he was 5 years old I bought him a quarter midget race car. He was in heaven. He was an awesome driver, a natural. As parents soon find out, raising kids is expensive. Of course, the first is always spoiled rotten with things you wanted as a kid and never had, but sure he wants one. You know, all the things they never play with but will rip your face off if you try and put it in the garage sale. So anyways, my racing days came to an end so I can spend the money on the kids. Not by necessity at the time, but a choice. So I made my decision to stop one of the two off time things I enjoyed the most. A choice. A decision that would affect my life because it was something for me, but I thought my future fun enjoyed with the kids would make up for the loss of my own individual play time.

Back to the watching the race by myself. As time goes by, life happened. We had a son, we lost a child before birth, my wife then had a daughter. We had a second daughter that was not necessarily planned, but we wouldn't give her away for love nor money. My wife was diagnosed with MS. We moved. I couldn't afford the time or money to keep my son racing. Our fabulous Social Security System turned my wife away from disability benefits because they said her MS would improve within 12 months to the point she could go back to work so she wasn't eligible. Obviously Multiple

Sclerosis doesn't get better, but they seemed to think so. Yet these same people gave gracious disability to a 19 year old that I met for alcoholism. Not only was he too young to drink at that time, but I couldn't see him as having a giant work background for him to be eligible. My wife worked for years. The family not only lost her income, but MS requires very expensive equipment to deal with. She couldn't drive anymore, then she couldn't walk, and I was going broke. Without my in-laws being there for us, it would have been a REAL ugly situation. My mom and second step dad moved back to this area to retire, only to have his life altered by a stroke, which led to his death after bedridden for ten years, my mom to care for mostly by herself. I made another life altering choice. I started drinking alcohol heavily. I thought it was the way to cope. It was the way my mom was coping. That decision is the reason I watched the race alone. My son and I should still be racing and enjoying watching the races together, yet the closeness of a "leave it to beaver" family environment is forever destroyed by my drinking. His alienation of me was the same as my relationship with my father. My father was an alcoholic and skirt chaser that destroyed our little family scene. My first step dad was the same, except he was also verbally abusive to me. I grew up rather callused, as did my son. He enlisted in the Marines out of high school to get the mentoring he should have gotten from me. He didn't get a father figure to prepare him for life as he grew up. I think he was struck harder by my actions than the girls were as he was older and understood more. My wife stood by me even as her illness progressed, the girls, well, they are teenaged girls. They watch the races for the cute drivers. The wife does have a favorite driver and kind of watches the race, but she's not the "good ole beer drinkin Monday Night football buddy" that watches the race as an event.

That was not meant to be a sad story as a tear jerker, but a reminder that your sad story isn't the only one out there. It's also not the only sad story I've got.

People are abused, people die. This sad story is the direct result of a decision I made to drink alcohol. There was no person that put the bottle to my mouth forty years ago, nor was there a hand that swooped from the sky and took it away from me three years ago, no higher power that shined a light in my eyes to make me see. It was my decision to not drink alcohol for the last three years, as it is yours. Will I ever drink again? Good question. Yes I do in fact miss having a drink at dinner, a few beers when people are over to watch Monday Night Football. I DO NOT miss getting absolutely hammered chugging on a vodka bottle until I would black out. Black out, not pass out. That's how I totaled out our almost new van. I should have pled not guilty for the DUII. You see, I wasn't driving. How could I? I was blacked out. I had no idea I was driving. Hell, I made it twenty miles from home before I crashed. Now isn't that a scary thought. We sometimes create our sad stories to rationalize a reason to drink. Shit happens, drinking doesn't make it go away, but you do have the ability to make the decision to face life sober. Hadn't you noticed that the reasons that forced you into drowning your sorrows in alcohol are still there the next morning? I guess the next question in your mind would be; "How do I deal with life sober?"…..I can't.

15

I CAN'T. That is about the most negative statement I can ever remember hearing. It drives me nuts. There are some things in life that are physically impossible, but if you open your mind, you would be surprised at what you can accomplish. I can remember a class in school where we did a mind over matter experiment. It really worked. One person lay on a table. Two people standing on his sides, placing just two fingers on each hand under his body. One at his head, one at his feet, again, just two fingers on each hand under his feet and head, a separate person reading from a book. The lights were off in the classroom for better concentration. The person on the side began reading to the person on the table, telling him over and over that he was light as a feather. Then that person proceeded to tell the others that this person had no weight. This went on for about five minutes, when all of a sudden, the speaker said "Now lift". Without even thinking we all lifted this person straight up in the air with our fingertips. I would not have believed it at the time that it could be done, but I was one of them at his side that did the lifting, no weight, no strain. I am a believer that we can lift ourselves out of alcoholism, just as we lifted the kid off the table.

16

I was at a party one time, drinking of course, somebody said "I can't" to something or the other, I don't even remember what it was, but I yelled out "BULLSHIT", tell me something I can't do. Someone yelled out "you can't put toothpaste back in the tube." I laughed. They should never have told me I can't. I proved them wrong. I did it. Actually not a whole tube mind you. But I got far enough they gave in. It took a while, but it was an old trick my grandfather taught me to pack grease in wheel bearings for a car. So as far as I am convinced, anybody can do just about anything if they put their mind and will to it, and know where to get the help needed to accomplish the task. Had my grandfather not shown me how to work on cars, I wouldn't have had the knowledge to apply that trick and accomplish getting the toothpaste back in the tube, which brings me to my point. You CAN do it by yourself. All you need is self confidence and some help and you can become an ex-alcoholic. Now, how can you do this by yourself? With help?

17

Doing it by yourself with help. Though this may look and sound simple on paper, it's not. I believe many alcoholics think they are alone, different, and have a near total lack of self confidence. Many, such as I, have been bombarded all their life as to how worthless they are. Verbal abuse may in fact be more devastating than physical abuse. Before I offend anyone, I cannot say that I was physically abused so it's tough to relate, especially if it was in the form of sexual abuse. Oh I got my whippings with a switch or a piece of two by four when I was growing up. I can think back to those days and get pissed off about it. The physical pain from the smacks on the butt are gone, but the verbal abuse I received growing up from my first step dad still lingers in my self confidence, and this is forty years later, being told what a stupid, worthless piece of shit I was. If I go to AA meetings and tell everybody there I am an alcoholic, eventually I'd be convinced I am. In a new mode of thinking, by telling myself I'm an ex-alcoholic, I have convinced myself that I am.

By myself. When a person lacks self confidence they seem to get callused to the world. I know I did, and I've seen it in many others. By trying to ask for help only adds to the feeling of helplessness. Ok now, switch that around. Using the feeling of being alone can actually be an advantage in the long run. Some people are introverts to the point that they would be better off working alone. Groups are not always the right answer. Unfortunately, if you are mandated by the court to attend Alcohol counseling, you will in fact be in a class. When you find you can break alcoholism by yourself the rewards are greater. It makes you stronger knowing that you beat the statistics your own way.

18

I found that by trying to drink myself into acceptance I was in fact driving people away. Alcohol gives a person a false sense of confidence, when in fact all it did was take the inhibitions away. When you use alcohol to gain your confidence, you lose your self control and do things you know are not right. You know that queasy feeling you get at times in your stomach when you are about to do something you know is wrong, like lying, which is immoral, or jumping off a large bridge with just a bungee cord tied to your feet, which can have devastating results if something goes wrong? The thing is, by doing either one, you are the one that decides whether or not to go ahead and do it. Just because someone else got away with it doesn't mean you will. Remember the first time you drank alcohol? That queasy feeling was there, the anticipation, the fear of the unknown. But you made the decision to take that first drink. The sad part about alcohol is its ability to release your inhibitions, which made you think you could do things that you would not normally do sober. How many babies do you think came about because of that thinking? How many people got dead?

Conquering alcoholism by yourself simply means that you are ready to make the decision yourself. You do not trust your fate to an unknown higher power. You are simply gaining the confidence in yourself that allowed you make the wrong decision in the first place. You made a decision to become an alcoholic, and it didn't work to your satisfaction. Get over it. Figure out how to fix it. When you can believe in yourself to start making the right decisions and gain that confidence that you really are not the scumbag they think you are, then you can make the decisions that will change your life in a positive way. You will need help.

19

Counseling. Yes this is something that requires another person or persons to complete, but if you are the one who makes that decision, then you are ready to accept what the counselor has to say. If you are court mandated to be in counseling and have the wrong attitude, you do nothing but waste time and money. I was in counseling twice, the first time I was a good boy and dotted the i's and crossed the t's, but the attitude I had gained me nothing. I learned nothing, but I did complete the course. Obviously not successfully or I would not have gotten my next DUII, a return ticket to jail and a (mandatory) invitation back to counseling. Fortunately I had an awesome counselor for both of my counseling sessions, Christina. The second trip through counseling I had opened my mind and made the decision to pay attention. Christina had a ton of patience, and through both sessions of counseling I could see why she needed it. Not all counselors have this patience or concern and care for the people in the class. This is where I stress that you try and seek a counselor that you can trust and feel confident that they only have your best interest at heart. Of course, your best interest is becoming an ex-alcoholic. The importance of this was very evident when she took a week of vacation. Her replacement did her job well as far as I could tell, but it wasn't the same. Christina can talk to people and relate directly to them, one right after another, like a chameleon changes color in it's surroundings, not just producing today's lesson on a chalkboard. There are people who genuinely care to assist you with your decision to stop. Find them. If you are not comfortable with your counselor, find an avenue to switch classes or counselor. Otherwise, you are rowing the boat with one oar.

20

During my alcohol counseling sessions I would sit quietly and listen (most of the time anyways) and laugh to myself as to not embarrass anybody. Inevitably about every third to fifth session, someone would "see the light". "Now I get it." they would say, some even to the point of crying in front of everybody, making a big scene. In my first go-around with counseling I was suckered in and wondered what this big revelation was going to be like when I finally see it. I never did. My counselor and I were talking out of the normal class time on one occasion and she told me that when somebody has made a decision to get sober that I would see it. And I did.

If you believe that a higher power is going to swoop down and save your ass, more power to you. Everybody needs something to believe in. I believe that the decision to try and face sobriety is an informed decision. It wasn't until the first few sessions in my second go around with counseling that I made the decision that I don't want to drink like that anymore. I had to get away from my power drinking. You see, I still had my health, such as it was, and I still had my wife and family. It's amazing all the sad stories there are in this world, I heard them constantly throughout my counseling sessions, with most endings indicating their situation is hopeless. I figured maybe if I tried, I could keep my wife and family intact. That was an informed decision by me. I don't know if I would have survived without the persistence of my counselor and the wise way she dealt with each and every individual in the class. One thing I did notice, when I saw someone has made a real decision to stop drinking, Christina was on them like a vulture on a dead rabbit. One of the strongest indications that someone has finally come to their senses is that they stop crying about all the sad things in life, and start asking questions. They are seeking help. They are not looking for someone or something to save them, but they are asking out of concerns for themselves. Bingo!

21

As I sat through the counseling session, I learned to expand my thinking. In case you haven't figured it out, that is THE thing I'm trying to relate here. Questions would come up now and then that would really catch my curiosity. The first one to really grab me was "why do celebrities (or people with high profiles) only get a slap on the hand and we get hammered?" Man I jumped right in the middle of that one. My very first thought was how she was going to get out of that one. Christina didn't even flinch.

That question and her answer was the very one that got me to actually want to quit my alcoholic ways. Her response was simple. "Don't worry about them, worry about yourself." I thought that was a pretty cheap way to get out of it, until I gave it some thought. Here I am faced with jail time, family harmony in jeopardy, bills up the ass, possible loss of job, physical and mental illnesses cropping up (I lucked out, I only faced blackouts, bleeding ulcers, and severe depression) or any and all other maladies that stem from alcohol abuse. Geez, do I really have time to worry about the rest of the world? If I didn't get myself together soon, I would have no world to worry about.

No matter how many times I thought I had things figured out, Christina always came up with a new way to think about various situations. I guess that's why she gets paid the big bucks. (Right she says). There is only one problem. So much of her talents were wasted. I know the first time through counseling, I was wasting a chair in that classroom. All it takes is an open mind, and I'll be damned if you can convince an alcoholic that they don't have one. We already have the answers, we can take care of ourselves. Right? That is why we were invited to attend these sessions, and Christina is the counselor. Is she some form of higher power? The way I look at it, all creatures are a higher power than I am if they hold the answers to my questions or can teach me anything about life. You can even predict what kind of winter we are going to have fairly accurate by watching the squirrels pack away food, or watch the geese heading south. But let's get serious. She had to drive a car to get to work. She didn't float in from the sky above.

22

Quite a few years ago while I was working for a large company and the store manager at the time was a real people person. He loved people and wanted to see each and every one of the employees under him be the best they can be. What this gentleman did was take all of the employees in batches, and ran them through a two day course in the powers of positive thinking in the training room. That was a ton of payroll to sit through two eight hour days of watching videos and reading material. The man in the video tapes was a professional. He talked only of the potential each and every one of us has inside. And he taught us how to bring it out. He taught about comfort zones and how to get outside of them, how to make a new path for our destination. It paid off with the payroll the manager spent with the performance of his employees. I don't think there was anyone in that store that didn't grasp something out of that class. You see, the man in the videotape did this for a living. Major companies spend countless dollars hiring him and others like him to inspire their employees to perform better. I know it worked wonders for me. I started making informed decisions for myself. I reset my standards. I quit worrying about what my peers wanted and expected from me, and made decisions that would benefit me. I went from a blue collar worker to a white collar job. I raised my own expectations. I was really starting to have fun in my life, not stuck in the same ugly day to day routine. You see, all my growing days I was told I wouldn't amount to anything, and I wasn't. After that course, I felt like I could accomplish anything. I had the power to control my life and all was well. Then I lost focus. Along with the focus went my self confidence. Along with my confidence went my self esteem.

At that point, all I could see was the bad in everything. My eyes were aimed to the ground more, rather than looking forward. It is so easy to lose focus if you surround yourself with people that don't have the same goals as you do. Regardless of the situation you must tell yourself that you do indeed have the power to be successful. But, if you are not careful, you can get lost in the moments and succumb to others way of thinking. That is the powers of persuasion. We as a people are bombarded with the idea of drinking day in and day out, television through ads and various shows, magazines, billboards, etc. You can't get to the milk in a grocery store without passing the beer aisle. There is a reason for that. Booze is good money. I used to have a keg in a fridge out in the garage. I did the math, and after all expenses it came out to about 38 cents for the same sized beer I was buying at the race-track for $3.25. Now that's some serious markup folks. That's why we are attacked with advertisement. Now I could be wrong, but I don't think there are a whole lot of people who actually set out to drink enough to be classified as an alcoholic. Peer pressure, advertising, other people's power of persuasion over us, and loss of our own personal focus is enough to spiral out of control. Then it's like a snowball, the more you push it around, the bigger it gets.

23

There seems to be a certain stigma with alcoholics that is so tough to shake. A lot of people say "Once an alcoholic, always an alcoholic". Of course I don't believe that crap. Now. I did. You see, I was normal. I would see some of them now and then. We all have. You know, the ugly scumbag on the comer with a cardboard sign scrawled with "Need $1 for food, please help." He hasn't shaved for a week, or bathed. The clothing they are wearing should be burnt. Sometimes we see men and women in groups of three or four, shopping carts full of old beer and pop cans. Of course we all know what they are going to do with those cans. Cash them in and buy more booze, right? That's why most people won't give them a dollar. Have you ever thought that maybe they do need food? We are alcoholics, branded for life in the old way of thinking. Typical pieces of shit. Don't waste a buck on them. If I had help making my mind up to stop this flaming spiral I created, and if someone gave me some focus and determination then maybe I could have avoided that crash. Go ahead and say it. "They've tried a thousand times to get me stop drinking and I can't". Of course they can't. They can't make that decision for you. You are the one that has to make that decision.

I was one of those people who would drive by and yell out the truck window "Hey asshole, get a job!" You know what's funny (not now) is that on my way home from work I'd see a bunch of scraggly men and women standing outside our local counseling center. They would be outside smoking a cigarette waiting for class to start. I'd laugh at all the losers standing around and sometimes wonder where they came from and how they got that way. I would also be looking to see if anybody I knew was there.

When I reached towards the lowest point of my life, I'd drive by after work, stop at the liquor store, grab me a pint of vodka now and then, and wave as I drove by them. It got worse. All of a sudden, an occasional pint of vodka now and then turned into a daily routine. Then it got worse. It got to the point I would break out in a sweat when it came close to closing time at the liquor store and I was asked to work over to finish a job. I guess by now I should tell you that I'm a beer drinker. Now my wife didn't care if I had a couple beers after work, but if she knew I was adding vodka to it, I'd have caught all kinds of Hell. My body got so used to the beer, it wouldn't get me where I wanted to go, so I added (not switched to) the vodka to do a better job. It did the job all right. What's nice about the pints I was buying was they started to make them out of plastic. They had a slight curve to the bottle that fit nicely over the transmission hump under the carpet. Plastic bottles don't give that tell tale clinking noise either when you're cleaning out the truck on your day off. I'd have to do that now and then because I'd run out of places to hide them. Then it got to the point that in the parking lot of the liquor store, I'd bend down low, crack the bottle open, take a huge swig, and THEN head for home. I'd have a little bigger grin as I went by that counseling center waving to the losers. By the way, this is the exact same counseling center I was court mandated to attend. Twice.

24

Until somebody has been there, they can't even comprehend how humiliating it is to be one of "those" people. You're hoping to God that no one you know drives by and see you. It's not that big a city, you can't hide. You can't smoke in the building so before class starts or on a break, you have to smoke outside. Outside naked for the world to see what a loser you are. It's surrealistic, like a bad dream, it's not me, I'm not one of them. Like the first time I got handcuffed and stuffed in the back of a police car after failing the sobriety test. When we got to the station, I blew a .28. For those who don't know, that number is from a breathalyzer. You blow into a tube real hard and they measure your blood alcohol content. At .08 they take you to jail in this state. As you do the math, I was three and a half times the legal limit to be driving. At .28, you're not that far from an alcohol induced coma. This also occurred in the morning, New Years Day as a matter of fact. And I was driving. Obviously not very well, as I spent that evening in jail. In jail. In a fog. It was cold. No blankets in the holding cell. I did get treated to a sandwich and an orange. I'm sure the sandwich was left over from lunch. Probably a day or two prior, that's what it tasted like. Dry wheat bread, enough mustard to give it a yellow tinge, dry bologna, slice of white bread, mustard color on about half of it, some more bologna, then another slice of white bread. The last bread was bare naked. It also had fallen halfway out of the little sandwich bag, so the top half was REALLY dry. The orange I think was from the season prior. This fine food made me want to come back for more. Right. But, it was food. I knew this couldn't be happening because I am not one of them. Like I said, in the thirteen months I was at my low with my drinking, I did just about all you can imagine. Went to jail. Went to counseling. Went to Jail. Crashed our van. Went to jail. I got my first ride in an ambulance from my house to the hospital, but I don't remember it. I even woke up in another city in a facility where they force you to dry out for a few weeks. Detox. All of those thirteen months are a blur. I'm not even sure the exact order of events, but my wife and kids probably do.

25

I'm not turning this into a graphic riches to rags, puking parts of my guts out, lost my job, ended up in the gutter type of story. I just wanted readers to know I have at least some experience in alcoholism. But this isn't about me. It's all about you. We all have a sad story. Some handle it, some turn to alcohol. The events or reasons I turned into an alcoholic are not important. Neither is yours. What is important now is what you are going do with it. How do we get out of the stigma of being one of "them?" This stigma is the one placed on those bums on the comer holding up a sign begging for money. Where do we go from here? We can either die by the river in a makeshift home under one of those blue tarps, or we can pick our ass off the ground and get some help. It's our decision.

I lucked out and still had a family and a home, so it was easier for me than it is for some people to get my shit together. And don't think for a second the word "easier" means this quest to be an ex-alcoholic and sobriety is going to be easy by a long shot. But there is hope. And in fact, you CAN reach the light at the end of the tunnel. In the counseling class, I'd listen to some of the people talk about living on the streets, in a halfway house or whatever. We all have a story. But if you look at them when they talk, you can tell the ones that want help, and the ones who have given up. The sad eyes looking at the floor most of the time when they talk are the lost souls that know not where life is taking them. Life is over as far as they are concerned. No hope. No where to go. The ones that look up with hope and ask questions are the ones who are going to make it. I was absolutely dumbfounded listening to my fellow classmates. I met people who had from nothing to their name but the clothes they were wearing, to the gal in "drydock" I ended up at that told the group that she and her friends could pop out $600 a day on drugs. Damn, what I could do with $600 a day.

26

What I wanted to accomplish here is just plain talk with the less fortunate. I know more about that subject than a $600 a day habit. When rich people go to rehab, they are gone for a while due to an illness. When the less fortunate go to rehab, they are drunken losers. But who are the losers? The ones who had little or nothing that fell into alcoholism, or the "influentials", the ones who can actually afford a $600 a day habit and became "ill" for a while? Poor people drink because that's the only way they know how to cope. Rich people have a three martini lunch, because they can. So who can you find at the country club swirling the green olives around in their martinis? There you will find your doctors, lawyers, maybe a few store owners or CEO of a major corporation, or maybe even the judge that sent you to jail. On the outside these two classes of people are totally different. On the inside, we are human, flesh and bones. If we are all the same inside, then why do the rich get off with a slap on the hand and the poor people pay through their nose for the rest of their lives? How many times have you seen celebrities get busted, drunk out of their mind, driving, get into crashes, causing public scenes? Then three days later you see them on TV in a fancy club hosting a party for all their friends, drinking $300 a bottle champagne. A poor man would be in jail, paying fines he couldn't afford in the first place. The flip side to this thought is that you usually see the rich "snap out of it" more so than the poor. Would that reason be the fact that the upper crust have more to look forward to? We don't need to worry about them anyway.

In order to move forward, it generally helps to have something positive to move forward to. Does it not stand to reason that the celebrities would be more apt to get their act together due to their higher profile? The amount of incentive to move forward comes from what is waiting at the end of the quest. To this point I believe a lot of people get their expectations too high and wish for change too fast. There is only one result in that way of thinking. Failure. I don't know that many people who are comfortable with the simple things in life. I think we as a whole all wish we were rich, important, smart, good looking, popular, or any combination of these. Lower your standards. We are starting from scratch again. As in a song, when we hit rock bottom we have two ways to go, straight up or sideways. How far up we reach for is something that should be determined by us as individuals. The stigma of an alcoholic seems to put boundaries on what they say we can expect to achieve. If we give in to that form of thinking and settle for less than we want from ourselves, then we truly have failed. Don't walk around telling everybody what you were. There is a certain sense of pride that shines when we can say "this is me" and not be ashamed of the past, and let others see you for what you are now. Today is now. Not yesterday, not tomorrow, but today. I would rather meet somebody for the first time and tell them what I am today, rather than induce an impression in their mind that I was (and probably always will be) a loser.

27

Wouldn't it be nice to laugh again, play with the kids, answer the phone, get some bills paid, square up with the IRS because you weren't sober enough to do your taxes for the last four years, or maybe just a nice dinner with your significant other? Then get off your ass and fix it. You broke it and no magic wand or higher power is going to physically pick up the phone and ask for help. If someone has to pray to a higher power to give them the strength to lift the phone and start pushing buttons, then let them pray. Even then, if one relies on a higher power to physically motivate them to change they are making the decision themselves to accept this form of assistance. I think the biggest problem there is the expectations of those higher powers to fix life for them, not give them the strength to help themselves. By asking for the assistance of a higher power to help break the grip of alcoholism, isn't that really your decision? It is our decision how we get there, and when we do decide, that is when the ball starts rolling. NO ONE CAN CHANGE YOU OR MAKE THE PROPER DECISIONS FOR YOU.

28

They can throw you into jail, or they can throw you into any type of counseling, but you will not change unless you decide to. Whether you believe in prayer or believe it is merely an informed decision, it doesn't matter. As long as you pick up the phone and push the buttons. Not many phones dial themselves.

I learned a lot in counseling. The main things to achieve in counseling are focus, determination, and help finding answers. And the nice thing about it, it's right in front of your face and it's free. Actually, the determination and focus we already have inside, it just needs to be found. If you have a yacht to go to from here, fine. If you don't, well that's fine too. It's just going to take a little longer to get your yacht. It may be a 12ft aluminum boat with a putt-putt motor, but it's your yacht, and you earned it. You will have just as big a smile on your face as the people in the speedboat that almost rolled you over in their wake. Don't be jealous, they aren't getting anywhere you aren't going to go, we all die. If I say it a thousand times in this book your reading, I still can't make it clear enough. It's your decision to be pissed off at the world and self-destruct, or make the best of what you have.

29

Now, let's say you and a buddy take one of those fishing trips in Alaska. You know the one where you fly into the boondocks because you can't get there from here any other way? Your pilot gets killed by a bear and now that bear is coming after you. The fact that neither one of you has flown a plane before is irrelevant at this point. Who's going to try and get that plane in the air and away from that bear? If I make the decision (and it's my life) then I'm going to be the one to get us out of there. Chances are we are probably going to end up crashing anyways, but I want to have the controls over my life. If I crash that plane, I might survive. I'm sure as hell not going to put my life in the paws of that bear. And I'm not exactly sure that my buddy can get me home any better than I can. I'm going to decide my fate. Moral of the story is, before you take a trip with alcohol, you might want to familiarize yourself with that bottle you're flying. Alcohol is just as dangerous as trying to fly a plane when you don't know how to control it. We just have to hope that if we crash, we survive. And if we survive, we should know what to do or not to do next time we make the decision go on another trip like that. We also have another decision we can make. Don't go on that trip at all. You can get fish at the store.

30

When we continue to call ourselves alcoholics, it's like carrying around a snapshot of someone you loved, dead, in a car wrapped around a telephone pole. Any time we look at it, we can see nothing but the ugly scene of a car crash. We crashed. Should we be doomed to carry the stigma of a loser for the rest of our lives? Why would we want to be constantly reminded of the ugly scene we created with alcohol abuse? The day your dear friend died in that crash, you were at the scene where they hit. Long black skid marks on the asphalt. Big ruts in the dirt all the way to the pole, glass shattered and spread around. Along the ground you see pieces of chrome, plastic, a kids doll from the back seat. When you return four months later, the evidence of anything bad that happened in this spot is gone. They say time heals all wounds, as did the rain that washed away the skid marks. The weeds grow straight and tall again, covering the ground and the telltale signs that a tragedy happened there. So how long do we need to keep that picture to remind us of what happened?

At first, I packed that picture around for a long time. That picture held the faces of my wife, my kids, relatives and friends. Daily I would punish myself for what I had done. Here I was trying to convince myself on a daily basis that maybe my first step-dad was right. Maybe I am the piece of shit he said I was. My self esteem was in the gutter. I have never done so much tiptoeing around trying to atone for the damage I had inflicted to everyone around me. As we live day to day reminding ourselves of our shortcomings, then we will be that person, day to day. All of a sudden it occurred to me. I spilt the milk, but I didn't kill the cow. And if the cow is not dead, then maybe I could refill the glass with milk again.

I am not an extremely patient person. I'm not sure what I was expecting people around me to do or how to act, but in a little while, I got tired of trying to atone. Trying to keep clean on a daily basis is nothing but a daily reminder, so why not just drop it? The tire marks are gone, the grass is back, and there is a new telephone pole up where the broken one had been. I can't undo what already has happened, but the sun will still rise tomorrow. If you died tomorrow, would they lower the flags to half mast? Nope.

31

I wrecked my family van when I was drunk. It was a black eye to who I was. My whole world was injured. The status of being the responsible one of the family was gone. This was a personal tragedy of biblical proportions to me. Then I see a commercial on TV for a life insurance outfit stating there is a traffic accident every five seconds. While I thought my wreck was an earth shattering event to me, it was nothing to the insurance company. To them I was just another statistic, and a small stack of paperwork. Our goal to become an ex-alcoholic is just as much a mechanical repair as getting your crashed car repaired. Things get bent and broken. Throw away the non repairable parts, fix what you can, paint it, then move on. Unless someone crawls over, under, and through your car, they would probably never know it had been wrecked. Let's say that now I want to sell that car. I have no intentions of putting a sign in the window that reads ~$600 or best offer, previously crashed.~ Now, if they asked me, I would not deny it, but I'm not going to go around telling everybody due to the fact that few people want anything to do with a previously screwed up car. That's why I won't continue to call myself an alcoholic. The only ones who want anything to do with an alcoholic is another alcoholic. They have no one else that wants to deal with them. They have that stigma. They are losers.

The technology for car repair is phenomenal these days, generally fixing it as good if not better than the factory. I have yet to have some stranger walk up to me and ask me if I am an alcoholic, and I sure as hell am not going to go around telling strangers that I was unless they asked me for a particular reason. I'd rather people judged me by what they hear and see from me, not the label glued on my forehead with the stigma of a loser. We have enough challenges.

32

So what is the big deal about going to an event where alcohol is served? I have yet been invited to a function where it is mandatory to drink alcohol as part of the festivities. If someone asks you if you'd like a drink, what's wrong with saying "Sure, I'd like a cola please." If they want to push it and ask if you'd like anything mixed with it, it's simple enough to say, "Not right now thanks." Why would you intentionally provide the information of past mistakes? "I'm an alcoholic, so I can't drink alcohol." All you are doing at that point is placing the sticker on your forehead that says, "I'm a low down drunk with no self esteem." The party is over for you at that point.

33

If you think that you could handle a drink at a function, then have one IF that's what you want. Just remember that it is an informed decision as to how the rest of the night is going to go, along with the next day, or even the rest of your life. Before we go taking a sip of alcohol after what we have been through, we need to make damn sure that we can handle it. So you really think that you can handle it. But can you? What if you wake up in the morning in bed naked with a stranger. Or worse yet, your best friends spouse or one of your in-laws? What if the Dr. says that a baby is now involved a couple of months later? Can you handle that? Before you even think about answering any of the previous questions, make sure you are 100% sober. It seems that answers to questions vary with the amount of alcohol in your system. Think about your answer today, sober. Then ask yourself how you think you would have answered these question two or three months ago when you were drunk at a party.

If you are not sure that you can handle just one drink, then be on the safe side and don't. If that queasy feeling is in your stomach when you are offered a drink, it's trying to tell you that maybe you aren't ready and it would be a bad idea. I believe that if you have in fact convinced yourself that you have beaten alcoholism, you won't have that queasy feeling anyways like the first time you ever drank alcohol. Remember, there is in fact a difference between an alcoholic and a person who drinks alcohol. As a matter of fact, I feel there should be SOME queasy feelings. These feeling are the ones that should be responsible for you to stay on guard and protect yourself. I used to get the jitters every time I strapped myself into my race car. Here is this machine that was specifically built to race and face as many adversities on the race track they can throw at you. The more safety equipment you strap on, the more confidence you have that you will survive the race, even to the point that you don't think about getting hurt at all in that car. You just want to race. But some race car drivers do die each racing season. It's a fact of life. Shit happens. It's a dangerous sport. So is drinking alcohol.

34

Other than the health factor to consider is the cost of alcoholism. If you think about it, a majority of serious alcoholics are on the poor side. Although we must remember that alcoholism knows no boundaries, male or female, rich or poor, ethnicity, age, or any other factor you can think of, a big chunk of them are poor. They drink because they are poor, and they are poor because they drink. This is one of the most vicious cycles a lot of alcoholics have to deal with and they don't know how to break it. One of the things alcohol does for you is provide you with a "Don't give a shit" attitude. The results of this type of thinking can be devastating in various ways.

First let's talk about the obvious. Cash money. How much money have you spent on booze? You know the stuff you are supposed to pay bills with, feed the kids, those kinds of things. Face it. The first of the month comes up and rent is due, gas bill, electricity, credit cards, insurance, cupboards need food, daughter was invited to a birthday party and no money for even a little something to give as a gift, empty gas tank in the car, court fines, and you find yourself a little tight. You are pissed at the rich people, afraid the phone will have another bill collector on it when it rings, so you unplug it. Depressed at the fact that you have to go through this again, not only this month, but probably next also. Ashamed your kids have to go to school looking the way they do, embarrassed to buy groceries with food stamps. This is a lot of emotions to have to deal with. So what is the obvious solution? Get drunk. Makes sense doesn't it? Spend the money on booze. Now that you have gotten the "Don't give a shit" attitude back, things are better. Right? They really aren't better; we know that, we just don't care anymore. At least until you wake up and have a few sober thoughts. Then comes the old saying, "I can't". I can't deal with this anymore. I can't deal with this sober. There, now you just gave yourself another reason to drink. Wasn't that easy? Here is where you have a choice. An even tougher one. This is where you alone are going to deal with the decision to face life drunk or sober. NO ONE ELSE CAN MAKE YOUR DECISION FOR YOU, YET SO MANY PEOPLE ARE AFFECTED BY THE DECISION YOU MAKE. Drink or don't. This takes us to the next consequence of your choice to drink in excess.

35

Family, friends or coworkers, or even the general public. Nobody is safe by the decision you've made to drink. The damage created by the decision to get drunk can be harmful physically and mentally to the people who surround you. Some people get to drinking and end up feeling giddy and happy. Some people drink and turn into real assholes. Some people get just plain stupid. Regardless of how one acts under the influence they are not themselves. It's the alcohol talking. No inhibitions, no smarts. Cheating with somebody else's husband seemed all right at the time you were drunk, then find out two days later he's at the bar bragging to all the guys about nailing you. Meanwhile the husband goes to that bar, finds out about the wife, gets violent drunk, picks a fight, and gets shot. Children have no daddy.

36

Have you any idea what the kids are doing or thinking when you are drunk? These are emotional scars that last a lifetime, a picture that can't be erased. The thing is they have a choice. Learn from you or copy you. Do you want them to be just like you? Everyone around you is affected, and so hard to convince you have changed. You are now faced with a lack of trust and a serious challenge to your sobriety. But remember, you made the decision to be that way, not them. So now it's up to you to make the decision not to drink and start mending some bridges. And also remember this, you are not going to mend them all so don't feel a failure if some of those bridges collapse. Sometimes it pays to build new bridges to get away from the people you got drunk with all the time. We are creatures of habit.

37

And now, look what you've done to yourself. Look at the living conditions you are experiencing now. What would you have if you were sober? Look in the mirror. Would you want to wake up and face that every morning? Everyone that shares your life does. Are you thinking as well as you should or is your short term memory shot? The first thing I experienced when I quit drinking was being scared. It is in fact a challenge to face life without a crutch.

A bad thing about using a crutch is you have a tendency to rely on it too much. Now you have to learn how to walk without it. You are the one that needs to throw that crutch away yourself and relearn how to walk. You were walking before you started drinking. When you were a baby and learned how to walk the first time, you had help and encouragement. It is still available to you but you have to make the decision to quit yourself. Kidneys shot? No, job? Are your eyes puffy and bloodshot? Red faced? Do you walk tall or cower? Are you physically impaired by the wreck you had when you were drunk, the one you don't remember? Do you still have the same expression on your face that you got when someone told you that you had killed someone? How about the you on the inside? Shame and humiliation come to mind along with embarrassment. How about the guilt? How many people are suffering from your decision to get plastered? How are you suffering from the decision to use alcohol to excess? How do I fix it? How can I face anybody again? How do I do it sober? I can't.....
BULLSHIT!

38

We were born, we crawled, we walked. Eventually we will die. Sometime in our lifetime we may stumble, stand up again and walk. Some of us run as we get wiser, but we are still prone to a fall. Those of us who get back up and run again will make it. There will be some that flat don't care. They won't. They more likely than not are going to die. Sad, but a fact of life. I have regained my focus on life, and I happen to be a strong believer that every problem has a solution. Although not all solutions to all problems have been found, there is very little as individuals we cannot accomplish. There are theories and methods of attempting to leave the alcohol abuse tendencies behind, but the successful will have two major things going for them. A positive attitude and determination. We really must believe that we can stop the alcohol abuse or it won't work. This is something that has to be physically dealt with by us, rather than waiting and hoping that someone or something else is going to fix it for us. Go look straight into a mirror. Take a look and see what kind of person is staring back. That is the only person that's going to convince you to stop the heavy drinking. Does the person staring back have the balls to quit? No? Then look at that person, stare right square in the eyes and chew their ass off. Challenge that person. Scream at that mirror until you are blue in the face. Don't leave that mirror until you have thoroughly convinced that person it can be done. If the person in the mirror believes that it's going to happen, it will. You will remain in the classification of an alcoholic if you can't convince the person in the mirror. Period. There is no pill available yet to do it for us.

39

By this point of the book, you are so close to making your decision on how you want to handle the alcohol abuse problem it's not even funny. Believe it or not, you're already halfway there. By at least thinking about it, you have started the focusing process. Remember, this is for you. Nobody else. Some of us will have to learn to crawl again, some will get right up and walk. The people with the best focus and positive attitude will be running again, soon. I think the quickest way to accomplish this is to forget the past. You have never seen that person in the mirror before, they have no past. So how long will it take to get back on track? It all depends on how hard you fell, but you will be on track eventually as long as you stay focused on the new life that has just been created.

40

Fear. That's the first thing I had to deal with. I would think of life being sober and wonder how I was going to pull it off and got scared. I could not focus. I had my crutch too long. What is interesting about me is I had my first taste of alcohol about 40 years ago. When I was about 11 or so I was running a tractor on my grandfather's property above the house. We had just got done plowing up the 5 acres and I was discing it to level it out. Of course it was summer, and hot. I had been discing for about 2 hours after lunch when I saw my grandpa walking out in the field with a sack. He waved me over and I shut the tractor down. Out of the sack came a cold six-pack of beer. He looked me in the eyes and said, "Danny, if you're gonna work like a man, then you can drink like a man." I had one beer then, and one beer after dinner. Of course it was out of my grandmother's sight. I grew up the next few years respecting alcohol. My grandpa was from the old country, a simple man. He was not an alcoholic. It was not until I was a senior in school living with my sister and brother-in-law. My brother-in-law was an alcoholic. Since then there is only one stretch of time I would rate myself as an out-of-control alcoholic. In that one 13 month span, I was arrested 3 times for DUII, one of them after I totaled out our van. That was over three years ago. Not a drop of alcohol since. That is how quickly one can fall, and how it is possible to regain focus just about as fast. The damage done in between can last a lot longer, but you can't fix anything if you don't get sober and re-focus.

The fear factor. How did I break it?

I made a decision. Not my wife and kids. Not my counselor. Not the police. Not even the fact that I was in a wreck that could have killed someone. You would think something like that would sober me up, but it did not. It was not until I was the one who decided when it was enough.

41

I got mad. No, I got pissed! I started thinking about my life growing up, and letting some jerk of a stepfather convince me I was no good. I thought of how I had pretty much beat those years of thinking from an intense two day class and moved forward. How life was good until I lost focus and didn't see the pothole of alcohol abuse, tripped and fell. How I was almost convinced I am and will always be an alcoholic. "HI! My name is Dan and I'm an alcoholic". "HI Dan!" BULLSHIT!

Forget it, it's over. That was a chapter in my life that came and went. I am moving forward. I made a mistake. I screwed up royally. I GOT OVER IT. That subject doesn't come up much anymore, but I will share it as a story of how alcohol can be conquered. If you asked me if I have done any drinking since I made my decision, I can look square into your eyes and say no. And I won't bring it up, nor will I ask you if you are an alcoholic.

42

Instead of whining about the mess I made, I started to face it. Not right away because it took my head a bit to clear. That fog lingered. It was kind of like when you get a major injury. This will be the time between when you got injured, took time to look at it, realize you did it, the numbness, shock, and finally the pain that sets in after the shock is gone.

Talk to anyone that you've had contact with when you were drinking so heavily. You'd be amazed at how stupid you were when you were drunk. I know I was. By talking with people I found out that I had said or done things that was either misunderstood or not appreciated. Take it on the chin. Suck it up. Apologize. Then drop it. Let them know that was in your past life, a stage that you went through. It was the alcohol talking. I believe once the subject is forgotten we can move forward at a quicker pace and gain more respect than if we keep hashing it over. By not whining about it shows others that maybe it is in the past and they don't have to tiptoe around in your presence. Don't even try to convince them it is. Convince yourself, and they will follow. I'm sorry to say that anytime we talk about those dark days, that sticker goes right back on our foreheads. The stigma returns. This world seems to have a tough time letting go of that title. Granted the withdrawals will remind us what we have done, but after a week or two, that will be over. The book on that life will close, so now we need to rewrite a new book. After the DT's were over, all withdrawal symptoms were gone and the whining about the mess I made, I started doing damage assessment.

43

Assessing the damage takes a little time to be thorough. I could not even comprehend how much damage I had done by the drinking like an alcoholic until I looked at my life sober. Deep in debt, I was behind in bills and accumulated court costs and assessment fees. Of course I had to attend counseling. We had to replace the van. I would guess you know what happened to my insurance rates. The kids were scared of me. The look on my wife's face about tore me in half. I could hardly even look at her knowing that in her time of need, while battling the Multiple Sclerosis and trying to hold the family together, I was drunk. The only reason I brought this up about my situation was merely to open the eyes of the people who haven't reached that point yet. This is just the tip of the iceberg as they say of what to expect if you don't break your alcoholism. If you think that sounds bad, I heard stories during counseling from others that made my mess look like a walk in the park. You don't want to go there. Trust me. Oh, one more thing about the damage that can be done with your head up your ass powering down alcohol., some damage you can't fix.

44

As I said I was in my second round of counseling already when I made my decision to quit being an alcoholic. Christina did not judge me. She allowed me to express my opinions and kept on providing answers to my questions. I learned. So I already had the first step mandated for me after facing the judge. I think he said something about counseling or jail. I needed help. If you are not already in one then you should look in the phone book or online for the nearest alcohol counseling center. Remember what I said about being comfortable with the treatment you are receiving or all efforts are wasted. Money. Most insurance plans will pay all or part of your treatment time. If they don't or you have no insurance, do it anyways. You will never invest your money into anything that will pay the dividends like counseling can; you are getting a whole new life back in return. Please note that I said a new life. The old life is over. Today starts today, not tomorrow, nor was it yesterday, it's today. We move forward from here. Right now.

45

One of the things that had me scared was the bills. Pick up the phone and start making calls. It's that simple. Their customer service number can be found on any of the statements in the sack full of unpaid bills in the corner by the kitchen table. One at a time, be honest with them. They would rather hear that you are struggling and wish to work with them rather than how you were pushing them off while you were busy drinking. A bad answer to a lender you owe money to is better than no response. Talk to them. They won't bite. As a matter of fact I found them to be more helpful than I anticipated. As I feared the worse, they made proposals for me to get back on track with them in ways that was even simpler and easier than I had anticipated. This simple step takes a ton of worry off of the shoulders and gives you a battle plan to get back on track. It also snowballs. Once you get the ball rolling back downhill again, it will pick up speed. It may also save on court costs if they plan to sue you. They will not go away. After contacting everyone you can actually start answering the phone again. It won't be necessary to screen the calls so someone won't make you lie and say the check is in the mail. If you don't have a job, get one. Don't let your pride get between you and the electric company. Take what you can get.

What I feared the most were the bills. They were too easy. No I did not have the money to pay them all, but I did in fact make arrangements with my creditors. That made them happy. That also took away the chills that ran down my spine every time the phone rang. The tough task is getting the family thing going again.

46

Again it was easier for me to get the basics back because my family was still with me. Some families get broken. Mine was when I was growing up. I swore I would never let my own family suffer like that. Bad feelings and bad memories is a poor mixture to use to make patches. Face it, some will accept you, some won't. When immediate family members leave the scene it's rather hard to find the support that makes you the most comfortable. Anyone can "sponsor" you, but is no contest for a loved one. Now don't take me as an expert on this situation, I was lucky to have family behind me. There are a couple of family members that won't have anything to do with me anymore and it's sad. But, the people that mean the most to me are still there. I am not a family therapist, so I don't have the answers. Find one if you need one. If you've been dumped by your loved ones, so be it. Worry about you first. They will either trust and work with you or they won't. There is no sense staying in a relationship that's not based on trust. Being cordial to each other is not the same as a real family. It may even put a serious damper on your quest for sobriety. Move on. Facing the aspects of starting over again in the family scene can be scary and depressing, but sometimes necessary.

I have not lived that situation, but like I said, going through counseling twice opened my eyes to a lot of different situations. I only got to see and hear about those stories. Other people had to live them. I just hope that if you find yourself in the need of this writing, you get your shit together before you reach this point. That is of course if it hasn't already.

Somebody out there is looking for a new life also. If your previous loved ones won't take back and accept you, then leave it be. They are not there. We need to concentrate on us. Let them take care of themselves. Don't get me wrong, be patient for a while. We left some nasty wounds to heal but it should be pretty obvious after a while. Don't force it. Stay focused. We have plenty to keep us busy with our own damage control.

47

Buy a new outfit. New shoes. Take a long hot shower. Get a haircut. Comb it a different way. This is today and we have things to accomplish. Look in the mirror when you're done. You don't have to be good looking to look good. Dress the part of a success and you will flow right into it. Stand tall, be proud. You are no longer an alcoholic. You are on track to being the person you always wanted to be. We can only reach as high as the ladder we choose. Failure is a state of mind, as is success. You are what you think you are. When you look for the positives in life, you will find them, and they will find you. My goal was to merely try and expand your way of thinking and to let you know that there are indeed alternative ways to beat alcoholism. The operative word in the last sentence was ~beat~. Follow the rules. Don't deviate and put yourself at risk of losing everything you wanted to attain. Punishment sucks. Then it's over. It's been over three years since my last court date. Probation, loss of license for that long, fines I had to pay, all add up to a pretty miserable life. Yesterday was my last official day of probation, but I'm not done yet. What I had done in my previous alcoholic life will take a bit longer to fix still. But by following the guidelines of probation, heeding the license suspension, any of the many things required to get my life back, I have come out of this situation with a few less boulders on my back. Don't try and fake it. I've seen people try. A person that is honest with themself and is truly committed to breaking the cycles of an alcoholic will soon be able to pull themselves out of the gutter. Don't let them tell you it's not possible, nor will I tell you it's easy. It's been three years since my last stupid stunt with alcohol and I'm not all the way out of the gutter yet, but dammit, I'm standing. And walking.

If you cannot change things where you are, have you ever considered changing where you are?

48

Now what? Do I really believe that it is so simple to change your entire lifestyle you have enjoyed for so many years? Not on your life, but if we continue to live our lives with the ignorance that we only have one option, not only is it not simple, it will be impossible for some. Remember that ignorance is not the same as stupid. If you are ignorant about something that just means you were not taught. Stupid is when you know something is wrong and do it anyway. The second and third DUII I got were from pure ignorance on my part. And who was to blame for that? Should I blame it on the counseling I received? They were full of information that they were instructed to pass on, and I'm the one at the time who chose not to pursue other options. The main reason for that is I didn't know there were any options. That my friend is ignorance. Now if I choose to get hammered again and risk what I have accomplished so far, that my friend is stupid. Anyone can change their ideas on any given subject at any given time as long as they have the proper knowledge to make an informed decision. We know that not all knowledge or paths to all situations have been found so if we cannot handle the information we have, maybe we should go out and find them. Do not be afraid to make a decision. If you make the wrong one, fix it and try something else. I think more people fail from not try-ing something new as opposed to being complacent where they are. I watched people in my counseling sessions answer questions with one mode of thinking but then change the tune of their voice if they sounded too frilly. Why? Because of the reaction of fellow students in the room. You know the ones I'm talking about, the cool dudes that are so laid back in their chairs with their arms crossed, the ultimate of cool. They give you the cold stare and shake their heads if you say something nerdy, like you are really serious about getting sober. That's ok though, most of them will be back in another session somewhere, soon. Or dead. I was given the return trip to counseling because of my attitude the first time. Thank goodness I didn't get dead first.

49

Paint a room. If you don't like the color after all when you are done, you have some choices. You can live with it, or repaint it. If you decide to paint it back to the original color, the process starts all over again. Moving things, covering others, taping edges, mixing paint, all the processes that were required to make it the color it is now. It's the same amount of work as the original paint job, sometimes harder if the walls you painted were too dark. Changing an attitude or belief is pretty much the same thing. If we go back to the way we were before we started drinking like fools, we have lived with that certain belief or attitude before, so we are familiar with it. We know what it looks like already, so why would we be afraid to change back? I think it stems mostly from the don't give a shit attitude induced by the alcohol. This attitude gave me a confidence to say and do things that I wouldn't do sober, but I didn't care. I was Superman on alcohol. Then I chose to face life sober. That takes a real man. Or woman. Right now I couldn't give a good tinker's damn what people thought of me. Once I brought out and fixed the real me, I found an acceptance from most people (close friends, relations). The rest who have met me for the first time will never get to see my past. I refuse to put that sticker on my forehead.

I guess we have spent so much time with the color we have been looking at for so long we have forgotten what it looked like before. The color I would like to be looking at now is the color of my life without debt, a life without a record. A life without the guilt of the way I treated my wife and children, a life of respect that I used to carry. I'll paint as many times as it takes to get it the way I want.

Soon I will have a life with a driver license again, three years with having to rely on your feet or someone else to get around sucks. I keep reading in the paper of people continuing to drive while suspended, uninsured. Do you believe that these people have made a decision to get their act together? I don't. A commitment is just that. We broke the law. We pay the fine. We do our time. But then it's over. We can start out fresh. Why can't some people suck it up and fix things? Sure it's a pain in the ass to be punished. The thing is, when it's over, it's over. Starting fresh with a clean slate is an awesome feeling, no more looking over your shoulder.

50

This is not made up, I promise you. I read in the paper the other day, some gal was in court in front of the judge being sentenced for her dealings with drugs. Evidently she didn't like what the judge had to say, so she ran out of the courthouse, jumped in a car with a friend, and proceeded to try and outrun the cops. I guess you can figure the end results. Her and her girlfriend ended up in the hospital after she put the car into someone else's garage, without permission or the doors being open. Thank goodness there weren't kids playing in the garage at the time. Now how smart is that? I've been in some really fast cars, but I'll be damned if I have been in one that was faster than a police radio.

When I was working as a mechanic years ago, and this is true also, one of the younger kids came back to the shop from lunch and asked one of my buddies if anyone was supposed to be in his car. He had an MG or similar little convertible. It was one of the few days in Oregon without rain so Alan had his top down. Alan grabbed about a 10 inch knife out of his toolbox (dull for scraping gaskets, but the bad guy didn't know that) and with another buddy, the three of us went up to the upper parking lot to see if someone was in fact there. Alan reached over the door and had a hand full of hair on the bad guy and put the knife to the dude's throat. The guy was trying to hot wire the car and take it. Why? According to the mall security guys who talked to the sheriffs that took him to jail, this dude had a court date downtown. For car theft. He didn't have the money for a bus. Just how stupid can people be? Pay the fine and do the time. What kind of life would you have if you actually did get away? Or are you going to be one of those dumbasses that get out of jail and go right back to what you were doing? Let me ask you something, do you usually get drunk or high before you try to pull a job like that? A little liquid courage will help you get the balls to do it again. It will also get those butterflies out of your stomach and give you super powers. You just had better hope the owner of the next item you try and steal doesn't own a gun.

51

What we are trying to accomplish in the scheme of things is a chance to live a life without having to look over our shoulders all the time. Assuming you got your drivers license back and are legal again, how do you react to a police car coming up in the rear view mirror? If your first response is something like "Oh shit" then what does that tell you? We must remember that we pay taxes (or should) so we are the ones that make the payroll to put these police on the streets. Anyone that is pissed at the cops has a problem. We hire them to protect us, sometimes from ourselves.

What would you think if a car came down the street, drifted to the curb, jumped it and hit a tree in your front yard? The first thought would be," Please don't let one of my kids be between that drunk's car and the tree." Your second thought would be "Where in the hell are the cops when you need them?

Will the boss find out you got busted again, remember that you are on probation? Not if there isn't anything to be busted over. If they gave a random urine test, will you be sweating bullets waiting to find out the results? I'm a believer that if we make a genuine commitment to clean up and live life again, we can take all our guilt, shame, humiliation, pain, sorrow, any mix of feelings we have thrust upon our self and stuff them in the toilet and flush it.

Do you realize the commitment you have made once you pulled the handle? Have you ever tried to get something out of that toilet when it is finished flushing? Have you ever said something to someone that you regretted, but can't take it back? There is nothing you can do at that point. Apologize, ask forgiveness, and move on. Even if they don't forgive you, don't let it ruin your life forever. Proper etiquette says we should apologize, maybe even atone for the bad things we have done.

But there is a time to move on. If they can't deal with it, too damn bad. This is the only life you have my friend, live it for yourself under your own rules. You have made a decision to pull the handle and move on. There are some things in life we don't want or need to come back and it takes courage to make the decision to lose it, because we have had it so long that we are not sure what to do without it.

52

Now. Let's discuss what I mean by living for yourself under your own rules. We spent a good deal of our time being taught the ways of life. We were taught the rules, and the consequences if we broke them. Then we are sent out of the nest to fly on our own. Sometimes in the flight of life we end up in surroundings unfamiliar to us, so we need some guidance to figure out how to deal with these new surroundings. If what you are facing is unfamiliar and seems wrong, trust yourself to know why there is that queasy feeling in your stomach. This is your life, so why would you let someone else influence your decisions? Chances are the wrong decision that you make is going to land you in jail, not them. We can ask ourselves why we can't live our lives the way we want to. The thing is you can do anything you want, you just have to live with the consequences. Not everybody gets taught the same rules. But remember, the surroundings you find yourself in will indeed have rules, and they will be dictated to you from the majority of the people in those surroundings, right or wrong.

You are free to believe the rules are wrong and do things your own way, but would it be wise in the present surroundings? Life as we know it can be totally different from our neighbors in a foreign country. If we choose to visit, it is up to us to be able to adapt and fit in.

53

There are people in this life that cannot read. They cannot write. There is no formal education in their life. So what if they are not taught right from wrong? They are probably going to make mistakes. Generally when we make a mistake, we find out real soon that our behavior is not acceptable. It's how we react to that situation that will dictate our success in the future. We can cuss the laws and the officers that arrested us, but if you stop and think about it, the first brush with the law is fairly forgiving. After realizing how drunk I was the first time I was arrested behind the wheel, and the damage I could have done, I should have sought out the cops that arrested me and thanked them. Unfortunately, I was not in the frame of mind I am now. I was pissed. They disrupted my life. When I was in front of the Judge, the punishment he dealt to me felt like I had committed murder. What I wasn't thinking at that time was, I could have.

The question is asked. "So I magically transformed my life in my mind, what will I be like tomorrow?" If you are anything like me, scared. Do you want to know one of the things that scared me? How people will accept me. We learned early in our school days that it is easier to go with the flow. There were a few dorks in the class that knew right from wrong that refused to go with the flow. They are usually the ones that got beat up at recess. They are also the ones who probably sent you to jail.

Maybe they are the ones who patched your body up after wiping out your car during a drunken rampage. These may be the same people who tried to save the life you took in the same accident. And just maybe one of these people was taking care of your children while you were in jail. I was so concerned as to how people looked at me, and I couldn't imagine facing anyone sober. I knew I had a lot to say, but I didn't have the balls to say it soberly. So for a long time I kept quiet. I had just gotten my ass smacked with a rolled up newspaper. I was so ashamed of how I treated my family but I found out something else right away. The human body cannot be abused by alcohol like mine was without something bad happening. I went through withdrawals, and I'd say a good week to a week and a half. They were rather harsh withdrawals at that. The shakes, headaches, poor sleeping pattern. I'm not getting graphic because I'm sure you probably have been there at least once. Besides, you brought it on yourself. Suffer the consequences. Nobody is going to hold your hair out of the toilet while you are puking, you need a shower anyway. And by the way, you won't believe how good it feels when you get beyond that phase.

54

What never made sense to me was the fact of how good drinking felt. The more I drank, the better I felt. Until the next morning. How many times have we woke up somewhere strange and swore we would never do it again. Another thing. How can we drink so much liquid the night before and be dying of thirst the next morning? That right there should tell you something bad is happening. When we wake up about to puke and have a jackhammer going inside our head with a headache rivaling a migraine, we pray for salvation, take a half dozen aspirin and go to sleep. That has the makings for a rather unproductive day. The thing is, I don't think we try hard enough to get to the next step. You see, it is too easy to cure that hangover with a $3.45 pint of Vodka. We pretty much think that once we are beyond the withdrawal stage we've got it licked. At this point, we have barely started. If this is really your first attempt at being sober, hang on. You're going for a ride. This is usually the point where people show their true colors as far as their commitment to shaking alcoholism. Speaking of shaking, the easiest way to get rid of the withdrawal shakes that you are facing is a good stiff drink. That will stop the shakes in a heartbeat. Or you can try not drinking alcohol for a few weeks, the shakes should pretty much be gone. Nobody said there is an easy way to break alcoholism, and a stiff drink will only stop the shakes. It won't stop the problem. I've tried.

55

I'm not going to go day by day. Each person has their own circumstances, and your health is a big factor in the way we shake this. What we have to face is going to be different from somebody else. There is no ABC 123 method to escape the grips of alcoholism. I also am not a believer that a twelve-step program can do it for you. Or a fifteen step. Or a twenty, or a six. I believe there is one step you DO need to take. A step to decide for yourself if you want to quit or not. Then anything you do after that to break your alcoholic ways that works for you is fine. Again in this respect I was so very lucky. I made the decision to stop my alcoholic tendencies before I killed someone or did irreparable harm to my own body, at least that I know of so far. I would have to say that going through withdrawals has to be better than going through the realization that I killed someone. How do you get past that? You have to have a really cold heart to shrug off that one. But if you are going to stay sober, you cannot allow it to be an ongoing self punishment. Being punished is depressing, just like the alcohol. Man, you think you sunk to a low by what you've done, just think about adding alcohol to your wounds. What else can possibly be done at this point? You will be serving time and have plenty of time to think about your next life, the one after prison. Here are where one decides to place the previous you into a history book. Here is where you decide if you want to get your head out of your ass again, or not. Especially if it was someone we knew, or even worse, our own child. But in real life there are people that have to face this. These people have crossed a line and can't go back. These people may never clear their head of what they have done, and they will be in jail a long time thinking about it. These people have a choice if they do get out. Some won't recover from the guilt and go dive right back into the bottle. They are probably going to die.

Drunk. But then can you blame them? What kind of life will they have when they are out? Will they get immediate social acceptance? Nope. How about a good paying job? Doubt it. How about respect? Not a chance. Some will get out of jail and spend the rest of their lives trying to atone for the damage they did. Some will write books.Some will put on seminars trying like hell to keep others from ending up where they did. I was forced to listen to some of these people while in detox, but the words went in one ear and out the other. Why? Because of my attitude.

The attitude I'm talking about is the one where we think we are different. We can handle it and don't need to be told what to do and how to live.

56

What I didn't realize is that they weren't trying to teach me anything, merely relating the consequences paid by drinking, both mental and physical, and where to get help. If I wanted it. We have heard it before, some whiny cry baby dribbling tears talking of how their lives were ruined by alcohol. You don't think those tears are warranted? These are lives affected by a decision from someone to become an alcoholic, not someone who had a drink with dinner. Say you are in a car accident, and you are driver A. Driver B runs a stop light. You collide and driver B dies. What is the difference from you going home from a tragic accident, or going to jail for manslaughter? Generally a good stiff drink, in other words, any alcohol in your system.

Were you impaired? Doesn't matter. Alcohol was in your system. This is where the stigma of alcoholics kicks into the max, and Driver A is a matter of circumstances. This is why we must be able to separate ourselves from alcoholics and someone who drinks alcohol. As I stated earlier, I had gotten 3 DUII's within a thirteen-month period. The circumstances surrounding that era of my life are unimportant to anyone, because I now have the stigma of a lowly alcoholic. It's been three years since I have consumed any alcohol. Let's say even a year or two from now if I had one or two beers, not impaired, under the legal limit, and something happened. Even at no fault of my own, I'm going to get hammered by the law. A first time offender will probably get sent to diversion, even blowing a .28, and receive probation as it was the first time I was busted. Now I would be headed for prison, by blowing a .08. An informed decision on your part will keep you from being one of these people. Alcoholism can be broken. Don't let anyone tell you it can't. Nor is it required to beat yourself up on a daily basis in front of other people telling them that you are an alcoholic. I admit that I was in fact an alcoholic, and I truly believe that I am no longer. Just try and tell that to the judge.

57

Cassius Clay, aka Muhammad Ali. He was the greatest fighter of all times. Who said so? He did. I'd bet when I was watching him fight I had heard him say that at least a thousand times as he would hammer that into Howard Cosells' microphone. Was he really? He thought so. And more often than not, his opponent would think so at the end of a fight. He told himself he WAS the greatest. Now throughout history that's what he will be known for. The man had a vision as to what he wanted to be. I believe if you put the same concentration and focus on becoming an ex-alcoholic, you will in fact be that person. Ali was a public figure. He had to convince everybody else who he was. We only have to convince ourselves who we are.

My idea of concentration and focus is probably different than most people might think.

My idea is to merely focus for a while of what you CAN do sober as opposed to what you have been doing while enjoying alcohol. Try writing things down that you can do sober. Open your mind. Think of things like waking up in the morning without a hangover, in your own bed. Having breakfast with the kids instead of fellow inmates. Having a driver's license to get to work, and if you get pulled over while driving, it's for a bad tail light bulb rather than a weekend pass to jail. It's inevitable. If you drive a motor vehicle, odds are you will get into some kind of accident sooner or later. Wouldn't you rather be the sober one, with insurance? Doesn't it do your ego wonders when someone calls YOU up for assistance? You can fix dinner without passing out and burning it or the house down. You can actually go pee without it ending up all over the floor because you are aiming at only one toilet. Isn't it sad that you actually have to stop and think about simple things like that? The thing is, we are creatures of habit. It does not take forever to get you into any kind of pattern. Good or bad.

Whether it's a pattern of stopping by the liquor store on the way home, or walking in the same door after work and taking off your shoes and put them in a certain spot, things we do just start becoming a habit. Look at some guys' levis and you can clearly see which pocket he puts his wallet in. It's the worn rectangle on the right rear pocket. Every day he gets up and puts a pair of pants on, and the wallet goes in the same pocket without even thinking about it. Would you like to make him go absolutely nuts? Sew the right rear pocket shut and make him put the wallet in the left pocket. All day long he will be walking around thinking that he has ten pounds of jagged rock in that pocket and then he will feel naked on the right side. This is exactly how it's going to feel without alcohol in your life. The only difference is those jagged rocks are going to be in your head. After a couple of weeks, that dude will put his wallet in the left pocket without even thinking about it or knowing you ripped the stitches out of the right one. You will too. That's the point we need to reach with drinking. When you're thirsty, all kinds of things besides alcoholic beverages will come to mind. Why? Because if you do something or act some way a few times on a consistent basis, it just comes natural. A habit. Now if you pick up an alcoholic drink, it will seem weird. Good. Let your common sense and that queasy feeling in your stomach dictate what your next move is going to be. You know what the consequences will be if you drink it. So if you go ahead and drink it, then it will be an informed decision. No one can stop you or make the decision for you. It's how you feel about yourself now, and knowing what you will feel like if you do. If this informed decision allows you to have that one drink (if that's what you want) and enjoy yourself without going overboard and losing control, then good for you. If you are not sure, don't even try. To be honest, I'm quite sure that I could enjoy a couple beers now without feeling the need to get hammered. Two things though. Number one. I'm still on probation for a little longer. Number two, at this point I would actually need a reason to drink alcohol, where before it was just a daily habit.

58

For me, now, not getting hammered daily is a way of life. It can and will be that way for you if that is in fact what you want for yourself. I don't even think about drinking anymore. Why? Because I'm in the habit of a lifestyle that doesn't include alcohol. And when I do think of alcohol, it's been so long that the allure seems to have disappeared, at least to the stage I left it. This is the point that I call the break-off point. You have broken the alcoholic's cravings. I consider this as being the final step that counts as your stopping point. From here on out, if you drink again then it will be an informed decision. When we are hungry our body tells us when we are supposed to stop eating. When we are thirsty, our body tells us to quit drinking, we have had our fill. What point do we have to reach before we are done with jail time, public service, hospital bills, being shunned by friends and family, loss of job, or any other consequence that can be thought of by overly stupid drinking?

59

Am I a creature of habit? Terribly so. At work I would grab a Snickers bar at my morning break to carry me over to lunch. Every single day at about 10:15 a.m. my body would go nuts if I didn't get that Snickers bar in me. Every day except for my days off. I had a totally different routine then. It was vodka instead of a candy bar. My body no longer demands either one. You will get that way soon if you give it an honest chance.

Eat well. Get outside and get some exercise. In detox there were more than a few who were sucking down coffee with about 6 packs of sugar in them, and this was all day long. You should have seen them panic when the coffee pot ran out, they were only trading highs. Prioritize your time, go ahead and write it down. When I have a list of things to accomplish I can get them done in a flash, even impressing myself. If I don't have a list I can spend the entire day trying to figure out something to do. The sad part is I would fill the gaps of boredom with alcohol. It is truly amazing what can be accomplished during the day, rather than driving the porcelain bus and popping aspirin until we pass out.

60

Here's something to try. Make a birdhouse. We can always find scrap wood laying around somewhere. Now you're going to say that you have never built a birdhouse before. Well guess what, just like the break from alcohol, we learn as we go. There are no blueprints in front of your face but with a piece of paper and a pencil, you can draw whatever you would like to see in a birdhouse, or what the rest of your life is going to look like. The only requirement for this birdhouse is a hole big enough for the bird to get in. As long as that bird can get inside and stay reasonably dry, it couldn't care less if the corners aren't perfectly square. The only requirements for your life plan is a hole big enough to park that don't give a shit attitude. I don't believe those birds care what color that birdhouse is, at least I never heard them complain about it. Hang it up on the porch and they will come to accept this token of your labors as their home. Get out in life. Soon people will accept you and your token of labors to be an ex-alcoholic. As with that bird, pretty soon the new person you became will be second nature, just like the bird's new birdhouse. What's neat is the fact that you built it, with your own plans. So now you say you have never worked with tools before. Neither did I until I picked one up and started using it, and do you know what else? Ask the person who sold those tools to you. If they don't have a clear answer on how to use it, find someone who does. There is usually a good reason that person is working there. Another good question that can be asked. Where do I get the money to work this change? Add up how much money you spent on booze, and if you are a cigarette smoker like me, you will probably smoke less, and cigarettes are pretty spendy nowadays. If you happen to be one of those idiots that also do illegal drugs, excuse me, any drugs with alcohol, don't forget to add that cost. Wouldn't it be nice for your kids to come home from school to a new bike, rather than a mother on the couch passed out?

One more thing you might try. Help a friend out. I guarantee that if you were an alcoholic, you know others that are also. Birds of a feather flock together. Look them square in the eyes and convince them they can get through life sober. When they can look back at you squarely in the eyes and tell you they are ready, make them repeat it a few times. You are the drill instructor, drill it into them. To see another individual change for the better merely reinforces your own efforts that you have applied to yourself. With yourself you feel the change, but you can't see feelings. With someone else going through the same transition, you can physically see the change. That pretty much seals the deal in the fact that you have felt it, you've seen it, and you know it works. You have just verified your efforts on yourself through someone else. Have you ever had company over and they had a baby? When the baby cries you usually want to do one of two things. One is to slap it on the butt and tell it to shut up. Or two, you want to make it laugh. Isn't it neat when you get them laughing again? It makes you feel good also, and everybody in the room is less tense. The same works for an alcoholic.

61

If in fact you do wish to continue to be an alcoholic, I guess that's fine too. Nobody but you can make that decision. Just do the world a favor and take it somewhere else. I don't give a shit what you do in that case, nor do many other people. I can't help you. Counseling can't help you. Only you can make the decision to help yourself, and you have to want it for yourself. I don't care if you are a famous celebrity or a bum under the overpass. You are no different, just different clothes. Only after a decision made by you to help yourself will anything anybody else say or do work. You can lead a horse to the water, but you can't make it drink.

62

I just want you to think on your own. Make an informed decision as to what is best for you. Why do people feel the need to let others dictate what to think or how to act? The simple reason is the want of humans to fit in. If we would concentrate on ourselves instead of trying so hard to be something else for someone else, maybe we wouldn't have so many of the pressures that drove us into the ways of an alcoholic. We all have pressures in life, whether it boils down to the proper wine we order at a fancy restaurant, or where we are going to find our next meal. The celebrities have it made don't they? Three hundred dollar champagnes, popularity, status, a heated bedroom at night. Then why should they become an alcoholic? They have it all. Maybe it's like when I was racing. When the races are over and the car is on the trailer in one piece, and there is a trophy on the hood, I am happy. I would drink to celebrate. If I got back to the pits and see the car in a bunch of pieces, I would get pissed and drink my troubles away. Celebrities have pressures like anyone else, and they are no smarter than anyone else that has fallen to the ways of an alcoholic. Alcohol doesn't give a damn how much money you have in the bank, or what your social status is. But there is this big fact of life that covers every one of us, we all have a choice in how we handle the way we act. Of course we all know there is an exception to every rule, physical or mental impairment requires a different path for assistance, they need to be going down a different road. That is where I say we need to do a little better job at the assessment before treatment.

I want you to think about one more thing. I won't tell anybody "Good Luck!" Luck doesn't have a damn bit to do with anything, especially breaking the grips of alcohol. You are in control (or should be) of your own decisions and destiny. You create your own luck.

Instead of getting hammered at a party to enjoy yourself, have a glass of wine with dinner and relax. Spend some time with the kids. Less people will die that way. You may even live a longer life. If a twelve step program works for you, great. If it doesn't, try something else. Take an alternate step.

It's your decision.

978-0-595-39782-2
0-595-39782-4